# LAWS OF THE CHURCH

## St. Dagobert II,

*King of Franks*

**Translated by:** D.P. Curtin

Dalcassian
Publishing
Company

PHILADELPHIA, PA

ISBN: 978-1-960069-72-6 (Paperback)


Library of Congress Control Number:
Author: Curtin, D.P. (1985-)

Front cover image: Portrait of King Dagobert II of France, 1738, Johann Georg Wille
Book design by J.J. Ripplestick

Printed by Ingram Content Group, 1 Ingram Blvd, La Vergne, Tennessee

First printing edition 2020.

# Introduction

The memory of our cultural consciousness is relatively short. In France today, when people discuss the national saint, they usually draw up the image of the great St. Louis IX, King of France, who was renown in his piety. Or, if not him, Joan of Arc, who was canonized by the Catholic Church in the 20th century. Little memory is paid, or remembrance made, to the other King of France has been canonized a saint- Dagobert II.

While still an undergraduate at Villanova I had discovered Dagobert II, the long-forgotten Merovingian monarch of early France. Little was written regarding his reign, and those things that had been written were blotted out by the hysteria of the faux historical 'Holy Blood, Holy Grail', made worse by the inane (but exceedingly popular at the time) 'DaVinci Code'.

The real Dagobert, and the political landscape that he lived in, was a nuanced figure, attempting to stride the world between the fragments of the memory of the Roman state, and his own Germanic tribal tradition. His administration had to navigate the seemingly endless civil wars that took place in Frankish Gaul, as well as the rising power of Frankish nobility. His exact relationship with the church is unclear, as some account claim that he was often in conflict with the bishops of his realm. Nevertheless, there was enough of a folk memory of his piety to inspire a cult of martyrdom around him starting around the time of Charlemagne.

What is clear from these texts is that he was a regular sponsor of the monastic communities in his realm and sought the protection of certain monastic lands through the grant of special privileges to the church. It is perhaps the heirs of these monks that helped promote the cult of St. Dagobert, who's estate they could lay claim to in continuity because of these royal charters.

D.P. Curtin
August 21, 2020
Glen Mills, PA

## I. The document by which Dagobert gives the baths across the Rhine, in the village of Auriac, together with their appurtenances to the monastery of Weissenburg - the year of Our Lord 675

Dagobert, king of the Franks, to the men of illustrious leaders, counts, domestics, or to all agents [in the nations], both present and future. We believe that this will stand for the stability of the kingdom, or for the remedy of our souls, if we bring to effect the petitions of the priests, [in] which they have revealed to our ears. Therefore, let your greatness or nobility know, because we, at the suggestion of the venerable man Ratfrid, Abbot of the Weissenburg monastery, grant those baths across the Rhine, situated in the village of Auciacensi, which Antoninus and Hadrianus, once emperors, by their work they built, to the monastery which is called Weissemburg. It was built in honor of St. Peter, in the village of Spire. We were seen to have agreed with all, and with the march itself belonging to the baths, which comes from two sides as far as the river Murga, and from one front to the western side one rast, and from the other front to the eastern part six leagues, which the people of that place say there are three rastas. Therefore, we ordered this precept of surrender to be made, so that on this day the abbot Ratfredus aforementioned, or the fathers of the monastery of Weissenburg, and his successors, or the monks residing there, concerning the aforesaid baths which they call 'aquae calida' or the march to the baths themselves. They shall do what they should prefer, that is, to have, to hold, and to leave to their successors the firmest power in all things. And in order that this present authority may be firmer, we decided to strengthen it under our hand and ring. Given on the 17th day of August, in the second year of our reign.

In the name of Christ,
King Dagobertus

## II. Diploma of Dagobert on the foundation of the monastery of Horra - in the year of Our Lord 675.

In the name of the holy and individual Trinity. Dagobertus, by divine preordained providence, king. If we provide for ecclesiastical business and the interests of the servants and handmaids of God every necessity, and if we strive to contribute some benefit from our affairs, we believe that this will be unfailingly beneficial to the state of our temporal kingdom, and to the earning of the eternal reward. Let the energy of all the present and future faithful of the holy Church of God be found, because at the request of our beloved consort Queen Nanthildis, a monastery in the Treverica valley, built in honor of the holy mother of God by our daughter Irmina, and decorated by an assembly of holy nuns, out of our property in the village of Murlen, in the Marca of Burense. These are the towns: Machera, Cornihe, Baldebruno, Hildenesheim, Waleheim, Speia, Brunneche, with cultivated and uncultivated lands, vineyards, mills, meadows, pastures, forests, waters and watercourses, roads and inroads, exits and retreats, and whatever we had, we contradicted by legal authority. That is to say, the condition that the poor of Christ should have some support for the rest, and they could prepare for us the support of eternal life by their supplications to God. Furthermore, we want it to be known to our faithful, both present and future, how our dearest daughter Irmina received her allodium, which Laudun bishopric in these places: Ludusa, Ancia, Balbengei, Wartengei, with all the appendages justly and legally belonging to the same places, from her husband Hermannthe count, as a legal dowry. This is given for the remedy of her soul and that of her aforesaid husband, to the same monastery called Horreum, with forty abodes in the Treverica itself, situated in the valley, and outside the city. Of these towns: Ornava, Muntzenfeldt, Willarei, Routzuurt, Wintersdorff, Rubera, by our hand, with all integrity, contradicted it. Namely, on the grounds that the sanctimonials there, perpetually serving God and his holy parents, should not suffer violence to the same property of any person, great or small, but should always obtain food and clothing therefrom without any restlessness. That this present tradition, both belonging to us and those in the future, may always have a great firmness in the name of God, we confirmed this precept written from there with our own hand, and ordered it to be marked with the impression of our seal. Thus, this act is to take place in the year 645 of the incarnation of the Lord, indiction on the 4th day of the month of September, in the year of the reign of Dagobert. May you be successful in the name of the Lord. Amen.

### III. Diploma by which Dagobert grants three courtyards to the monastery of the Argentine church - in the year of Our Lord year 675.

In the name of the holy and individual Trinity. Tagebertus, by divine mercy, most noble king. Let it be known to all the faithful born and to be born in the holy Church of God, how I, King Tagebertus, bequeathed, with the will of Christ, to my own sons, holy Mary to me as an inheritance. I acquired an heir, giving, in honor of the same mother of the Lord, to the Argentinian church and monastery three of my best and chosen courtiers, whom I so distinguished from the rest as to preside overall. One of which is situated in a village called Bischovisheim, and in the county of Chilcheim. The other, in a village called Rubiaca, and in the county of Ilchicha. A third in a village called Species in the county of Bargense. Of course, these aforesaid courts to the aforesaid monastery, together with the servants, nobles, or even knights belonging to the same courts, were handed over by the right that every year of their lives the,y and their descendants, should give four coins as a legitimate tax to the same court in which they were known to abide within. The inferior servants I have removed from the aforementioned place, that they are to give twelve pieces of money. Excused from this are: those who acquire free liberal wives, so that their sons pay no tax, but still live by the same rights as their fathers. In addition, their ban should be the price of three solidi, except that if they happen to do something against the monastery, they will pay this according to the gratuitous will of the procurator of that place. Yet, the estates were not completely cultivated, nor did they properly consist only of the vine. Beyond this, I distinguished those who engaged discreetly with my servants from others, so that whoever was born of one of my servants, whether they were of the male sex, should not pay any tax. However, the age of the female sex, as aforesaid, pays the legitimate tax. After this, those who protest, by what counsel I may commend my body to God and his mother, as long as I lived, I promised to serve her as a grace, so that she would commend me to her carnally begotten son, our Lord Jesus Christ, on the day of judgment. Above all, so that the free people who had benefited from my courtiers, for the sake of persuasion, had promised to serve themselves in the same way as I, not servilely, but liberally, legally according to the law of men. So that they might request from me if they had ever done anything, they would amend this more easily by half than the rest of the free people, which I granted. Moreover, if they should have made any amends, by right of these advocates, with seven solidi and a half they should satisfy the praisers themselves, rather than by appointing the same advocate. And if any one of these is guilty of the greatest fault, he shall make amends with the greatest ban of thirty shillings. If the prince of the same place ever convinces any of these that he has committed any of these things against him by design or even by deed, he shall amend this as if he were a free man. If he wishes to become innocent, with the aforesaid law of the freemen, then he becomes blameless. To these free men, who by my persuasion had committed themselves to the same monastery, I established such a right that they should have the power to buy, hold, give, sell, and to pass on their own rights to their posterity, and no one should surrender them, except free men living in the same courts who would commit themselves to the same monastery by my advice, and surrendering themselves, and justice over all who are subject there. In addition, if there are any who come into the power of the same monastery living liberally in the third calendar of March, they shall afterwards protect themselves in the law of advocates and in the law of free men. Hence the aforesaid liberals should present no servants to the lord of that place or to the king, unless they had benefits from them. In this way also, that every man with a coat of arms should possess ten estates, and then every one of them should continue to send wherever they wished, with the food of the bishop or the king, by the very laudatory ministries of the three vicarages. If any one of them, not having benefits, is required to serve as the defender of that place, he shall continue in the service of defending the kingdom for a space of three weeks. These events took place in Isenburg; and in order that these things may be believed to have been done by us, and not be broken by our posterity, we strengthened with our own hands and commanded them to be sealed.

The sign of Lord Tagebert, the pious king.

I, Turandus, the king's chancellor, by his command, wrote back. These took place on the fourth ninth of April, the seventh moon, in the year from the Incarnation of the Lord 762, the fifth indictment, during the reign of King Dagobert, in the 32nd year of his reign.

## IV. The diploma by which Dagobert confirms the town of Germiniacum granted by his father Sigibert to the monasteries of Stabul and Malmundari - in the year of Our Lord 677.

Dagobertus, king of the Franks, was an illustrious man. We trust that this will come to us for the stability of the kingdom in the name of God, if we decide to confirm the deeds of our lord and progenitor Sigibert, the former king, for our utterances in the name of God. Therefore, the venerable man Goduinus, abbot of the monastery of Stabulau and Malmundarius, suggested the clemency of our kingdom, from our lord and progenitor King Sigibert. Saint Remaclo was from a town called Germiniacus, in the village of Rheims, to the aforesaid monasteries which are in Arduenna, which the prince himself built by his own work. This very town of Germiniacus, with all its integrity, its appendages belonging to it, that is, two mills under one roof. with the aria above the river Suppi, the vineyards in Beterio with the vintner, all this in its entirety to the very monasteries which are in honor of our patrons Sts. Peter and Paul, and St. Martin, or other saints who are known to be venerated there at the very places, by his precept. Wherefore the venerable man Abbot Goduinus, who had mentioned the law, and strengthened it with his own hands, brought it forth for us to read at the present time. He asserts that a part of the monastery itself appears to possess or dominate the very thing intimated above at the present time. Therefore, the whole matter demands our firmness, and we ought to confirm it more fully from this to the above-mentioned monasteries by our precept in the name of God. Know that he granted his petition, just as to each petitioner, and confirmed it in all things. For they oversaw this, as it is evident by the inspection of the precept of the aforesaid prince, the town itself intimated above, with all its integrity and solidity, had granted the border to the same. They grant this to the mill itself, the vineyards with the vinedresser, and in such a way that it was seen by his law to the very places of the saints. Henceforth by this precept of ours, both lands, houses, manses, manors, buildings, with vineyards, fields, meadows, woods, cultivated and uncultivated, waters and streams, more fully confirmed in the name of God, so that the equals of the aforesaid monastery may have, hold and possess this. Goduinus himself and his successors for a long time may be able to possess or dominate this. The monks who appear to serve there at the monasteries themselves, or the poor who are expected to receive alms at the very places of the saints, it is better for those chosen for the stability of our kingdom, to implore the Lord's mercy more attentively. In order that this law may be received more fully, in the name of God, for our own and for future times, with the help of God, we have decided to confirm the strength of our hands by signatures upon it.

Latin Text

I. Diploma quo Dagobertus thermas trans Rhenum, in pago Auriacensi, cum pertinentiis donat monasterio Weissemburgensi ( ann. 675).

Dagobertus, rex Francorum, viris illustribus ducibus, comitibus, domesticis, vel omnibus agentibus [ M. B., gentibus], tam praesentibus quam futuris. Illud ad stabilitatem regni, vel remedium animae nostrae perdurare credimus, si petitiones [ M. B., petitionibus] sacerdotum, quas [ M. B., in quo] auribus nostris patefecerint, ad effectum perducimus. Ideo (1302C)cognoscat magnitudo seu nobilitas [ M. B., utilitas, vestra, quia nos, ad suggestionem viri venerabilis Ratfridi abbatis, de monasterio Weissenburgo, balneas illas [ M. B., balnea illa] trans Rhenum, in pago Auciacensi [ M. B., Anciacense] sitas [ M. B., sita], quas [ M. B., quae] Antoninus [ M. B., Anthonius] et Adrianus quondam imperatores suo opere aedificaverunt, ad monasterium quod dicitur Weissemburg, et est constructum in honorem [ M. B., honore] S. Petri, in pago Spirensi, visi fuimus concessisse cum omnibus, et cum ipsa marcha ad ipsas (1303A)balneas [ M. B., ipsa balnea] pertinente, quae venit [ M. B., veniet] de duobus [ M. B., ambobus] lateribus usque in fluvium Murga [ M. B., Merga), et de una fronte ad partem occidentalem rasta una, et de alia fronte ad partem orientalem leucas [ M. B., leuinias] sex, quas [ M. B., quod] homines loci istius [ M. B., illius siti] dicunt rastas tres esse [ M. B., deest esse]. Propterea hoc praeceptum cessionis fieri jussimus, ut [ M. B. add. ab] hac die memoratus Ratfredus abbas, vel patres [ M. B., pars] ipsius monasterii Weissenburgensis [ M. B., Weissemburg], suique successores, vel monachi ibidem commorantes [ M. B., commanentes], de suprascriptis balneis quas dicunt aquas calidas [ M. B., aquae calidae] vel marcha ad ipsas balneas [ M. B., ipsam balneam] (1303B)pertinente, faciant quod [ M. B., add. ipsi] maluerint, hoc est, habendi, tenendi, suisque successoribus relinquendi firmissimam habeant in omnibus potestatem. Et, ut haec praesens auctoritas firmior [ M. B., firmiter] sit, manu nostra vel annulo nostro subter eam decrevimus roborari. Data sub die xj Augusti, anno secundo regni nostri. In Christi nomine Dagobertus rex.

II. Diploma Dagoberti de fundatione monasterii Horreensis ( ann. 675). In nomine sanctae et individuae Trinitatis. Dagobertus, divina praeordinante providentia, rex. Si ecclesiasticis negociis et servorum et ancillarum Dei utilitatibus (1303C)quaeque necessaria providerimus, et de nostris rebus aliquod beneficium conferre studuerimus, id nobis ad temporalis nostri regni statum, et aeterni promerendum praemium incunctanter credimus profuturum. Comperiat ergo omnium sanctae Dei Ecclesiae fidelium praesentium et futurorum industria, quia rogatu dilectae conjugis nostrae reginae Nanthildis, monasterio in Treverica valle, in honore (1304A)sanctae Dei genitricis ab Irmina filia nostra constructo, et sanctimonialium coadunatione decorato, ex rebus proprietatis nostrae in pago Murlense, in Marca Burense, has villas Machera, Cornihe, Baldebruno, Hildenesheim, Waleheim, Speia, Brunneche, cum terris cultis et incultis, vineis, molendinis, pratis, pascuis, silvis, aquis aquarumque decursibus, viis et inviis, exitibus et regressibus, et quidquid habuimus, legali autoritate contradidimus: ea scilicet conditione ut pauperes Christi inde in reliquum temporalia subsidia habiturae, aeternae vitae subsidia nobis supplicationibus suis apud Deum possint praeparare. Praeterea fidelibus nostris, tam praesentibus quam futuris, notum fieri volumus, qualiter dilectissima filia nostra Irmina allodium suum, quod Laudunensi (1304B)episcopatu in his locis Ludusa, Ancia, Balbengeis, Wartengeis, cum omnibus appendiciis ad eadem loca juste et legaliter pertinentibus, a sponso suo Hermanno scilicet comite in dotem legali traditione suscepit, pro remedio animae suae, et praedicti sponsi sui, ad idem monasterium quod vocatur Horreum, cum xl mansis in ipsa Treverica valle sitis, et extra urbem, istis villis, Ornava, Muntzenfeldt, Willarei, Routzuurt, Wintersdorff, Rubera, per nostram manum cum omni integritate contradidit, ea scilicet ratione ut sanctimoniales inibi Deo sanctaeque genitrici ejus perpetualiter famulantes, in iisdem bonis nullius personae, magnae vel parvae, violentiam patiantur, sed victum et vestitum inde semper absque omni inquietudine consequantur. Et (1304C)ut haec praesens traditio, tam sua quam nostra, stabiliorem in Dei nomine semper possit habere firmitatem, praeceptum hoc inde conscriptum manu propria subterfirmavimus, et sigilli nostri impressione insigniri jussimus. Actum anno DCXLV incarnationis dominicae, indictione 4, VII Kal. Septembr., anno regni Dagoberti ij. Treviris in nomine Domini feliciter. Amen.


III. Diploma quo Dagobertus tres curtes concedit Argentinensis ecclesiae monasterio ( ann. 675). (1305A) In nomine sanctae et individuae Trinitatis. Tagebertus [Dagobertus], divina favente clementia, nobilissimus rex. Notum sit omnibus sancte Dei Ecclesie fidelibus natis et nascendis, qualiter [quod] ego rex Tagebertus, exhereditatus [Dagobertus, exheredatis], Christo volente [voluntate], propriis filiis, sanctam Mariam michi in hereditariam [ deest apud Koenigsh. ], heredem acquisivi [accersivi], dans, in honore ejusdem matris Domini, ad Argentinensis ecclesie monasterium tres curtes meas optimas et electas, quas ita discernebam a ceteris ut preessent cunctis [ desunt apud Koenigsh. ]; quarum una sita est (1305B)in pago qui dicitur [ deest apud Koenigsh. ] Bischovisheim, et in comitatu Chilcheim; altera in pago qui vocatur [ deest apud Koenigsh. ] Rubiaca, et in comitatu Ilchicha; tercia in pago qui nuncupatur [dicitur] Species, et in comitatu Bargense. Scilicet has supradictas curtes ad supradictum monasterium, cum servientibus, optimatibus, vel etiam equitibus ad easdem curtes pertinentibus, eo jure tradidi [ut omnibus annis vite sue ipsi et posteri eorum quatuor nummos ad legitimum censum dent ad eandem curtem qua visi sunt degere. Sed viliores servos ita dempsi a supradictis, ut dent duodecim nummos, exceptis hiis: si qui liberales mulieres acquirant, eorum filii nullum censum reddant, sed tamen vivant eodem jure uti patres eorum. Insuper bannum eorum (1305C)sit precium trium solidorum, nisi si que forte faciant contra monasterium, hoc emendent secundum gratuitam voluntatem illius loci procuratoris; nec tamen omnino expertes predii, neque proprie vite consistant. Super hec, Speciensem curtim discrete (1306A)cum servientibus michi ab aliis ita discernebam, ut quicumque a famulantibus michi serviliter essent procreati, masculini sexus qui forent, nullum censum reddant; sed feminei sexus etas, ut predictum est, legitimum censum persolvat. Post hec demum cupiens querere, quo consilio corpus, quin pocius animam, possim Deo et genitrici ejus commendare, me ad idem nonasterium, quandiu vixissem, ejus pro gracia promisi serviturum, ut ipsa me in die judicii commendaret ex se carnaliter nato filio Domino nostro Jesu Christo, ac maxime, ideo ut liberales qui beneficia ab eis de curtibus ex me habebant, mee pro causa suasionis, se eodem modo quo ego, se promisissent servituros, non serviliter, sed liberaliter, legaliter jure virorum; petentes a me ut si (1306B)quid unquam fore fecissent, hoc facilius emendarent dimidie partis quam ceteri liberales, quod et concessi. Sed et insuper, si quid emendare debuissent, in advocati ejus jure, cum septem solidis et semis satisfaciant tamen ipsis laudantibus, quin pocius eundem advocatum constituentibus. Et si quis horum pro maxima culpetur culpa, si culpabilis sit, in maximo banno triginta solidos emendet; quin etiam, si unquam presul ejusdem loci quemquam horum contra se consilio vel facto etiam fecisse convincat, hoc emendet quasi liber vir. Si autem insons velit fieri, cum predicto jure liberalium inculpabilis fiat. Sed hiis liberalibus, qui se sua sponte pro mea suasione ad idem monasterium dederant, tale jus constitui ut habeant liberam potestatem emendi, habendi, dandi, (1306C)vendendi, et posteris eorum propria jura dimittendi, et nemo eos supradicat, nisi liberales in iisdem curtibus degentes qui se meo consilio eidem monasterio commendarent, et tamen ipsi supradicant, et justiciam inveniant super omnes qui illuc subditi sint. (1307A)Insuper, si qui sint qui in ejusdem monasterii potestatem veniant liberaliter degentes tercio kalendas Marcii, postea in advocati jure et in liberalium virorum tueantur; et hinc predicti liberales nullum famulatum domino illius loci vel regi exhibeant, nisi ex eis beneficia habeant; ita etiam ut unusquisque loricatus vir decem mansus possideat, et tunc pergat unusquisque illorum quocunque velint eos mittere, cum victu episcopi sive regis, ipsis laudantibus ministeriis trium villicationum. Si autem quisquam ex eis non habens beneficia exigatur in famulatum ipsius loci defensoris, trium ebdomadarum spacio pergat in servicio ad defendendum regnum quarta intrante, si ei nolit beneficia dare, fiat in presencia ejus cujuscumque velit miles. Acta sunt hec in Isenburg; et, ut hec [ea] a nobis facta credantur, et (1307B)a posteris nostris non infrangantur, manu propria roboravimus [roboramus] et sigillari jussimus. [Signum domini Tageberti regis pii. Ego Turandus, cancellarius regis, ipso jubente, rescripsi. Acta sunt hec] quarto nonas Aprilis, luna septima [decima], anno ab Incarnatione Domini DCLXII [DCCVI], [indictione quinta, regnante Dagoberto rege], anno xxxij regni sui [nostri].


IV. Diploma quo Dagobertus villam Germiniacum a patre suo Sigiberto concessam monasteriis Stabulensi et Malmundariensi confirmat ( ann. 677). Dagobertus, rex Francorum, inluster vir. Illud nobis ad stabilitatem regni in Dei nomine provenire (1307C)confidimus, si facta domni et genitoris nostri Sigiberti quondam regis, pro nostris oraculis in Dei nomine firmare deliberamus. Atque ideo vir venerabilis Goduinus, abba de monasterio Stabulau et Malmundario, clementiae regni nostri suggessit, eo quod domnus et genitor noster Sigibertus rex, S. Remaclo ex villa cognominante Germiniaco, in pago Rhemense, ad supradicta monasteria quae sunt in Arduenna, quae ipse princeps suo opere construxit, ipsa villa Germiniacum, cum omni integritate, appenditiis (1308A)suis pertinentibus ad se, id sunt, molendini duo sub uno tecto, cum aria super fluvio Suppia, vinea in Beterio cum vineatore, hoc totum vel ad integrum ad ipsa monasteria quae sunt in honore patronis nostri S. Petri et Pauli, et S. Martini, vel sanctorum ceterorum qui ibidem ad ipsa loca venerari noscuntur, per suam praeceptionem concessisse. Unde et ipsam praeceptionem memoratus vir venerabilis Goduinus abba, suis etiam manibus roboratam, nobis in praesenti protulit relegendam, et asserit quod pars ipsius monasterii ipsam rem superius intimatam tempore praesenti possidere vel dominari videntur; sed rei totius firmitatem nostram se petit, et plenius ex hoc ad suprascripta monasteria per nostram praeceptionem in Dei nomine confirmare deberemus. (1308B)Cujus petitionem, sicut unicuique justa petentibus, praestitisse et in omnibus confirmasse cognoscite. Praecipientes enim ut, sicut constat per inspectam praeceptionem jam dicto principe, ipsa villa superius intimata, cum omni integritate et soliditate sua, terminum ad eamdem, vel ipsa farrinaria, seu vinea cum vineatore, taliter per suam praeceptionem ad ipsa loca sanctorum visus est concessisse, et hoc ad praesens pares ipsius monasteria possedisse vel dominari videntur; ita deinceps per hanc praeceptionem nostram, tam terris, casis, mansis, mancipiis, aedificiis, cum vineis, campis, pratis, silvis, cultis et incultis, aquis aquarumve decursibus, plenius in Dei nomine confirmatum, ita ut pares praedicti monasterii hoc habeant, teneant atque possideant; et (1308C)ipse Goduinus successoresque sui perennis temporis hoc valeant possidere vel dominari, qui potius monachis qui ibidem ad ipsa monasteria deservire videntur, vel pauperes qui ad ipsa loca sanctorum alimoniae expectantur, melius eos delectorum pro stabilitate regni nostri, Domini misericordiam attentius exorare. Et ut haec praeceptio pleniorem obtineat, Dei nomine, nostris et futuris, auxiliante Deo, temporibus vigorem manus nostras subscriptionibus super eam decrevimus adfirmare.

The Scriptorium Project is the work of a small group of lay people of various apostolic churches who are interested in the preservation, transmission, and translation of the works of the early and medieval church. Our efforts are to make the works of the church fathers accessible to anyone who might have an interest in Christian antiquities and the theological, philosophical, and moral writings that have become the bedrock of Western Civilization.

To-date, our releases have pulled from the Greek, Syriac, Georgian, Latin, Celtic, Ethiopian, and Coptic traditions of Christianity, and have been pulled from sundry local traditions and languages.

## Other Titles and Translations by D.P. Curtin:

*First Book of Ethiopian Maccabees* (2018)
*Protoevangelium of James: Greek and English Texts* (2019)
*Edicts of the Synod of Paris* by Chlothar II, King of Franks (2019)
*The Life of St. Desiderius* by Sisebut, King of Visigoths (2019)
*The Synod of Rome* by St. Boniface IV of Rome (2019)
*Letter to Pope Theodore* by Victor of Carthage (2020)
*The Decree of 610* by Gundemar, King of Visigoths (2020)
*Laws of the Church* by Dagobert I, King of Franks (2020)
*The Old Nubian Miracle* of St. Mena (2021)
*About Fifteen Problems* by St. Albertus Magnus (2022)
*Testament of Some Former Things* by John Scotus Eriugena (2022)
*The Georgian Synaxarium* (2022)
*Instructions: Counsel for Novices* by St. Ammonas the Hermit (2022)
*The Syriac Menologium and Martyrology* (2022)
*Book on Religious Exercise and Quiet* by St. Isaiah the Solitary (2022)
*Vision of Theophilus* by St. Cyril of Alexandria (2022)
*On Fate (De Fato)* by St. Albertus Magnus (2023)
*Fragments of 'Chronicle'* by Hippolytus of Thebes (2023)
*Life of the Blessed Theotokos* by Epiphanius Monachus (2023)
*Syriac Life of John the Baptist* by Serapion the Presbyter (2023)
*Second Book of Ethiopian Maccabees* (2023)